HEMMING THE WATER

Hemming the Water

Yona Harvey

Four Way Books
Tribeca

for my family
and for my grandmother, Annie Laura Harvey

Please direct all inquiries to:
Editorial Office
Four Way Books
POB 535, Village Station
New York, NY 10014
www.fourwaybooks.com

Library of Congress Cataloging-in-Publication Data

Harvey, Yona.
  Hemming the water / Yona Harvey.
    p. cm.
  Includes bibliographical references.
  Poems.
  ISBN 978-1-935536-32-1 (pbk. : alk. paper)
  I. Title.
  PS3608.A78928H46 2013
  811'.6--dc23

                    2012029330

This book is manufactured in the United States of America
and printed on acid-free paper.

Four Way Books is a not-for-profit literary press. We are grateful for the assistance
we receive from individual donors, public arts agencies, and private foundations.

This publication is made possible with public funds
from the National Endowment for the Arts

and from the New York State Council on the Arts, a state agency.

NYSCA

[clmp] We are a proud member
        of the Council of Literary Magazines and Presses.

Distributed by University Press of New England
One Court Street, Lebanon, NH 03766

Contents

"... I didn't have no religion. But I didn't want my parents to look bad."
—Mary Lou Williams

"The resilience in you comes from your artistry. . . the way your mind is put together and the fact that you cannot desert your children."
—Ruth Stone

THE GATE TO THE WATER

SOUND—PART 1 (GIRL WITH RED SCARF)

There was a girl with a red scarf, a girl with a white scarf, a girl with a pink scarf & a girl with a scarf of pale pale blue. & when, from a corner of earth far from where the girls were born & far from where any of the girls then stood, their scarves unwound & snapped like ribbons or wild wild hair, it was the girl with the red scarf who stood apart from the others, though they all stood laughing wildly together. & there was talk of toads & talk of kissing & many gowns & much ceremony, but mostly talk for talk's sake away from too many ears curved to listen. Though listening is what the girl with the red scarf did most, which made her from a distance seem still, though she moved with the other girls or at other times with her brothers & sisters in a queue slithering onto the school bus or into the house, which was never still. & when at particular moments her ears were full of odd instructions & she needed to hear something across a room, she listened with the whole of her body, her eyes & skin, her hair, which was not wild but microscopically braided. Sound was God, as she understood it, always poised to listen. What does a girl with a red scarf hear? Only she knows, approaching the world from the inside in. The center of the ear: a drum. Rain on leaves. Fingers on books. On bellies. On windows. With a boy pressed against her, she attempted music, a collaborative first. An unsex. What was that sound? The naught-girl signal? Womanish gardenia opening? God is good. (Sometimes). Fierce fragmentation, lonely tune.

Blessing Blue Crabs

Smiling white teeth, television
      host pleased with her face, her
there-you-have-it filling the screen.
      One last shot of the elegant restaurant
poised a few miles across town, its proud-
      bellied chef & owner, spit-polished silver,
glasses clear enough to ring.
      Goodbye to the women who blessed
the blue crabs with hymns, who undressed
      the trapped bodies from once-blue shells,
lifted the meat from their legs, sealed
      flesh for markets, who weren't invited to
sit at the linen-clothed tables of the fine
      restaurant featured on the cooking program,
a "must-stop" for indulgent diners
      passing through the Lowcountry,
who, still in uniform, sang
      stridently in the cannery kitchen,
who spoke barely above whispers to cameras
      stationed outdoors for interviews, against
the backdrop of foamy sea, whimsical sailboats,
      who posed at picnic benches propped for the occasion,
supplied with paper napkins, who sampled
      the chef's famous crab cakes, a cup
of water to wash them down.
      Yes, they are delicious. What else
could they answer without accusation
      of ungratefulness, their dark fingers
shaking away the delicate crumbs?

To Describe My Body Walking

To describe my body walking I must go back
        to my mother's body walking with an aimless switch
in this moment of baptismal snow or abysmal flurry.
        There's a shadow of free-fall frenzy & her unhurried

the way snowflakes are unhurried toward transformation
        at my living room window. She moves unlabored, she
will not ask me to invite her in, but she will expect it.

        I will open the door to her. She is my mother,
even if she is made of snow & ice & air & the repetition
        of years. (A means, a ways).
She came out of trees surrounding me. I see her cross

        now the creek in her patent leather shoes, their navy
glimmer like a slick hole I might peer over & fall into,
        against so much snow weighing down the prayerful arms

of sycamores, which doused the bushes last autumn.
        Her little hearse broke down near the exit
that leads to my house. Now she must walk.
        She will be tired. I will let her in,

though she will not ask. She has come so far
        past the mud & twigs, the abandoned nests.
This time of year she can't tell the living from the dead.

The pathway is mostly still except for her moving
            with the snow, becoming the snow. Forgiveness?
She is a stamp in it, the tapping of boots
            at the porch steps.   Not spring.

Or summer. Just her advancing, multiplying—
            —falling through branches
                        —there's a flurry of her.

DISCOVERING GIRDLES

I don't know what to do with this contraption
of polyester & cotton, troublesome lace. Black,
white, another woman's nude—whatever the color—
its trick is to hide flesh, to constrict the skin
like a bit of truth, a secret buried in the garden
of women's undergarments. A prepubescent girl
signals her mother to quiet, to lower what must be
her first bra & yes, it's fine & can she go now?
My mother's concerns for me were body odor &
virginity—how to smell like a flower without being plucked.
Robust women filled her church, their stomachs
suffusing the linen of long dresses doused with perfume.
I do not know how to behave, publicly
contemplating these hip huggers that wouldn't matter
to those women, reaching beyond the fitting rooms of Earth.

Rose Lassi

It seems I would die if I drank
the extract of a rose. Liquid
petals, barely tamed fire
in yogurt. All the flowery dreams I dreamed
as a girl, stains that troubled
bed sheets the middle of nights, lipstick smeared
on a prom date's collar, wet
blossom of my dress crumpled on the backseat.
I taste the satin, the collar slipped
bitterly over my tongue. Kisses
exchanged, lovers' mouths, sex more
deadly than love, my
husband's wedding lapel in late
July, fascination with the red
bulb in his apartment before we married.
I am drinking the roses that bloomed
too late at the side of my mother's house.
We have a right to live in this neighborhood, her saying.

ALL MERCHANDISE SOLD AS IS: NO REFUNDS, RETURNS, EXCHANGES, GUARANTEES

A woman weighs the price of beauty—
hats, blouses & scarves in her bony hands.
She's draped in the dark greens of the sea—a sun-
dress—someone has sewn for her, the unlined
fabric hugging her pregnant belly, which floats
like a world beneath her long black hair.
She's the Goddess of Peculiar Patterned Blouses,
Our Lady of the Poorest Hour. Our Thrift Store
Blessed Assurance. New Orleans drifters,

stretch sweaty bills & loose change to style.
You get what you pay for. The sign says
in blunt red letters what the clerk doesn't care to repeat.

We choose carefully, we mothers stealing
Saturdays without children, dangling
skirts & purses in the stale light. We take
chances on blouses we'll wear brazenly
as middle fingers. No fear. No fuss, guarantees.

Sound—

Hair cranked up, voices cranked up, hands & necks snaked to shape
   the words.
Girls predict rain & raise Cain on campus on street corner, at movie &
   make-up

counter, each voice amped by the other, little luminous leaves egged
   on by fast winds,
ensuring wild, wild weather. When my mother spoke freely, echoes of
   her girlhood

rose from the Lincoln Courts, each playground chant. I listened, the
   way

old women listen to gods & spirits who visit. They pour chamomile to
   ease the spirit.
They give freely their ears, their tongues, then stop—

                              —mid-sentence—as if they shouldn't be speaking.

When my mother's mouth slipped open like a blouse, she lowered her
   eyes
& covered it suddenly. Salt-palmed, panicked, I braced the smart-
   mouthed & ornery

of English & algebra class, fought a similar silence. I've trembled
   among strangers

& lovers turned strangers, my small voice collapsed in solitary song. I
   sit
across from people in restaurants, clenching spoons, afraid of what we
   might say.

CHATTERBLUE

Sunday, your declarations of blue. The widening spell of sky, the faint
ink of curtains hampering your great, blue thoughts. Shouldn't we all
stop to note your blue mood, how it grips you like a pair of blue hands
that kept you as a boy & bids you speak fondly of your blue childhood:
I was loved, I was loved, as if you were the only one. The very blue air
takes hold of you like a blue capsule swallowed with a glass of blue
water, the capsule bursting into a million bulbs of blue light, its elixir
spurring you to cerulean fondness & shouldn't we, the people who are
supposed to love you best, love it too, or at least how your love causes
you to chit-chat, wagging your blue tongue, expunging your blue
breath—oh the breadth of the things you declare—& shouldn't we all
love as much as you who Friday went on about bodies in your dreams
trembling red?

TURQUOISE

& then the woman who wants
to sleep with my husband sends him a card
with Frida Kahlo's sepia
face peering through it & he
begins reading the note aloud to me, as if
the words might bring the woman back
across the line she crossed that summer
he mentioned her name for the first time.
Then I think his brush with temptation
isn't as noble as he'd like to believe, more like
cleaning the house when it gets dirty—he could
mark it on a table of triumphs, but, at the end of the day,
it mostly amounts to what he is supposed to do.
Men are so clueless sometimes,
which isn't a revelation, but occasionally needs restating
& brings to mind something I read
about Lenny Kravitz who composed penitent lyrics for Lisa Bonet,
how he believed the pair might reconcile
as soon as Bonet heard the album he'd dedicated to her.
I am clueless sometimes, too,
like the woman who cried to me on a campus bench
that she wanted to be an artist, to travel,
while the others rushed to lunch, to more classes.
& what should she do? Then I thought,

We are always asking questions whose answers
we already know & That's a great necklace she's wearing

which I told her, but she recoiled when I said
wearing turquoise jewelry & Frida Kahlo skirts
doesn't make women artists, which was probably the cruelest thing
I'd ever said to a young woman, but exactly how I felt
watching her fuss over the ruffles of her long, black skirt.
These days, Frida Kahlo appears
like a god to whom I've prayed,
like accessories that shake
at the bottom of a woman's shopping bag, a loose
divinity of feel-good postcards & magnets
rocking on paper handles in the crease of an upright arm.
This is what I think when I ask my husband to stop
reading the note he wants to render harmless.

Does a woman's affection for Frida make her
my comrade? Years ago, with my head wrapped & bracelets
jangling, I might have answered yes. But when I ask
Who's Lupe, Who's Frida, Who's Diego? I can't help but conclude
someone's at work on a grand cliché I'm supposed to buy into
& there's nothing harmless about Frida Kahlo, exquisite painter
of stitches & steel, thorns & wombs & vaginas—something utterly
misleading about Frida's face on a 4 x 4 note card, a little
too neat & too square, which makes sense in the American sense
of matinee love or lust or art or what passes for art, or living
the life of an artist, those heroes & heroines dangling over
the cliffs of vanity, begging for a little more rope.

MOTHER, LOVE

Because you are not April or June or January or
slush-caked boots or snow falling or melting or moving
in from the northwest plains, one cold coffee of a late

night, my bruise, my blade, my thorn, I love. Here
in the fold of a cramped journal, I've nothing
to whine about, to hate, or to feel indifferent to.
I write with the ink that is your name, dark

blood in the droop of a pale handkerchief.
When the baker runs her hands against the smooth
flour & sugar tins with their satisfied lids, she is
not like you. She is not your sewing

machine in danger of falling over the edge. No,
you're at least thirteen clocks in the span
of two rooms, each off by a minute or two.
Lord, help me when they chimed.

& so my love is awkward & ill-timed.
Here's the oversized window you
keep looking out of.
What trip are you planning, you

never punctual retired secretary, you
flat-ended film, you holy shock of self-absorption,
polyester panties, cotton knit pajamas, you
paper jam, you yesterday, you
Minister of Excuses, you tardy bell,
parcel package, unexpected visitor,
unanswered phone call, shout
from the basement, rainstorm,
static in the busted speaker, hearing
aid, headache, cabinet void of teabags
& measuring cups, passive-aggressive,
stomach ache, one & a half minutes too long, day
late, dollar short mother
of mothers, you
mother
you.

[ZODIAC SUITE]
—after Mary Lou Williams

[ARIES]

Elusive little g-o-d
Green shoot above frost
Air in crocus throat
& therein my mother
[My first My prayer My hurdle]

[TAURUS]

Liked to slip beneath
The snow & wonder
Liked to slip beneath
My coat & wander
Liked to slip beneath
His fists & weep
Liked to walk across
My wrists & bleed
Liked to gain a pound
To meet his match
Liked to lose a pound
To lose his kid
Crown me in red
Crown me in red

[GEMINI]

Eyeballs obvious
Watched & watching
Womb-mates
Vodka tonic
Treble bass
Half-note
Espresso
Terrible
Stutter
Stutter
One for my baby &
Over

[CANCER]

Bony legs heaped
Upon butcher's paper
Or—
Wooden houses
In haunted expanse
Planks exhaled
Shadowed & pillared
We wept in corners
Of the brightest rooms
Damn that city below the sea

[LEO]

The shock
Of your voice
Solo
Monk-like
Twinkle tooth
Diamond claw
Even in constellation
You a solitary star
Born thirsty
Born swinging

[VIRGO]

Real or imagined
I stopped what was coming
Before weeks curved
Before curves widened
Before confession
What did it matter
What I dreamt
I was no one's mother
No one's memory
No one's bride
There was nothing
Between the Lord & me

[LIBRA]

Track ten   with its sounds   of engines almost
Turning   was that your speed   your sadness
The keys   just dangling
dumb   beneath the dash
What are they   without
The jagged grooves   of love   in which to click
Or maybe   you await   a privileged kiss
All the joints   unhinged   & swept   in neat piles
Is that   your speed   your sadness

[SCORPIO]

when I came here   to be a housewife
I gave up my home   when you look
at the big picture   three weeks
are nothing   a second   a nanosecond
my days are full   of anyways
no big drama   no nostalgia   leaves
from your wedding bouquet
so this is how it is   to want
to tame the hour   to unveil
love's face   did you notice
this paper   has no lines
did you notice
your hair   has bloomed

[SAGITTARIUS]

No matter how the tube twists
The gumball clings to its path
Quarter + latch turn
A girl's cupped hand
Color sphere
Metal door swing
A Japanese summons
Anticlimactic exit
Waterfall
Water break
Tunnel bridge elevator airshaft
Attempts to direct
What the arrow [infant] feels
The infant [arrow] cannot articulate
Forward caught
Physics stricken
Bull's-eye shocked
Shivering
Against the matter fact

[CAPRICORN]

You are faint, they say
Eyes aslant
Not quite
What the Creator intended
You sang for the goats & the fishes
Nine-month speculations
Undone
No almost left to query

[AQUARIUS]

After the first hard strike
A rush
A running over
Is regret a fluid matter
Wedding cake
Ice pick
Bunsen burner
Highest flame
Most high priestess
Creek beneath the creek

[PISCES]

The waters still frozen   a child
        Peered through
Wintry   looking   glass
        All the armors
Glittered below
        Gold rotation
Amphibian flutter
        Gill breath
The Lake played the part of the Lake
The Snow played the part of the Snow.

Swimming Lessons

Sound—Part 2: Hearing My Daughter's Heartbeat the First Time

"kah doom / kah doom doom / kah doom / kah doom-doom-doom // the heart,
the heartbeat, the heart, the heart beats slow"
      —Etheridge Knight

"Now / I have beaten a song back into you"
      —Yusef Komunyakaa

"Furious music of the little drum whose body was still in Africa, but whose soul
sung around a fire in Alabama. Flourish. Break."
      —Zora Neale Hurston

            it's the girl

            in deep water
            who will not drown

                  (drum)
            come down

            (drum)

            come down

                  (drum)

            zora's instrument
            hidden in the belly

            (drum)

carried
across the atlantic

(drum)

it's a mystery to master

(drum)

it don't stop
                (drum)
don't stop

(drum)

gotta story to tell

(drum)

won't stop

(drum)

gold-black fish

(drum)

swimming

(drum)

an old one
come back

       (drum)
blood

(drum)

       breath

(drum)

       memory

(drum)

ka-doom   (drum)

       ka-doom

(drum)

ka-doom

THUMBELINA, I WROTE A SONG ABOUT YOU

You march on silk
You thread the bobbin
Keep the motor underfoot
Quilts & flags will ease the metal
Little tension never hurt
Bomb shells popping over yonder
Duty glaring overhead
Thumbelina, trace your pattern
Thumbelina, halve your yard
(Thumbelina bet not stop)
Thumbelina, mind your manners
Thumbelina, wind your watch
The Great Machine, you keep it oiled
Not much room between the stitches
Cut it
Pin it
Toss it
Hang
Walk big
Walk wide
When it rain
Anna Julia
Mary Church
Always ghosting in the sound
Thumbelina never tumble
Thumbelina always toil
A-line
Cuff

Sleeve
Who will wear it
Pocket
Patchwork
Pardon
Hem
Pushpins
Pillows
Weary
Dreary
Pulley
Incline
God's Machine
Maybe
Moving
Like a rail car
Keep your compass
In your pocket
Fight for wages
Mend the tears
Leave your wristwatch
On your person
Keep your coins
Travel lightly
Thumbelina
You steady spool of onward evening
Toss your legs upon the bed
Rest the capsules in the cabinet
Tuck the pistol near your head

Ocean Song

Who dreamt of drowning
in the blue robes? (Not
stars blanketing beaches,

not striped fish lapping water,
flapping their golden tongues.)

Who chased the women last night?
Where was God when they called
their sisters back from the dark?

One of them searched the numbers
& wrote a Zodiac Suite.

She found a monk in Arizona,
her desert water, her
black cactus, her

handsome faith. She found
Martín de Porres too. Children starved

as the ocean sifted its salt.
Who knows what to pray for? Who's guilty
of beginner's mind? What life is this

where even the strange feels cyclical:
the roar of waves in a seashell, stingrays,
pregnant corpses washed ashore?

Hurricane

Four tickets left, I let her go—
Firstborn into a hurricane.

I thought she escaped
The floodwaters. No—but her

Head is empty of the drowned
For now—though she took

Her first breath below sea level.
Ahhh   awe   &   aw
Mama, let me go—she speaks

What every smart child knows—
To get grown you unlatch

Your hands from the grown
& up & up & up & up
She turns—latched in the seat

Of a hurricane. (You let
Your girl what? You let

Your girl what?)
I did so she do I did
So she do so—

Girl, you can ride
A hurricane & she do
& she do & she do & she do

She do make my river
An ocean. Memorial.
Baptist. Protestant. Birth—my girl

Walked away from a hurricane.
& she do & she do & she do & she do
She do take my hand a while longer.

The haunts in my pocket
I'll keep to a hum: *Katrina was*
A woman I knew. When you were

An infant she rained on you & she

Do & she do & she do & she do

Even Disasters

wear white & turn
to honey. A hive

of bad hair days
swarms
inside me. Doom

is lessened out
of the public eye.

The welts, at least
won't show. Dressed
to the nines & too sweet

in the mouth. What
did he mumble?

Something
about insects
garnishing the frosting?

A baby
buried somewhere
inside the cake.

"The Antelope as Document"

1.
If I am the dove
& you are the wind
together we have some business.

2.
Maybe I'm a Little Half-Chick, one
of the lost ones on the way to Capital City,
thinking along the journey: I'm whole
& The King will be so pleased to see me.

3.
Erase the deities of ocean & sky:

4.
If you want to be touched, say, Touch me.
If you want to be held, say, Hold me.

5.
An antelope running wild on the plains of Africa
should not be considered a document.

6.
The girl's green t-shirt reads
SAVE DARFUR. Such a message,
how shall we classify? In the context
of a day without rain? Or in the neighborhood
the girl walks? In the borders of her country
strapped & declaring war?

7.

OBJECT	DOCUMENT?
Star in sky	*No*
Photo of star	*Yes*
Animal in wild	*No*
Animal in zoo	*Yes*

8.

(Coffin draped in flag	No)
(Photo of coffin draped in flag	Yes)

9.
Eventually, wisdom arrives—
But men spill their milk in the meantime.

10.
Who will offer his tongue?

SCHOTTELKOTTE

All our goodnights sound like matches striking.
Goodnight, grenade—little knock in the murk, little

pill in the palm. Put us to sleep
while we sleep. One B leads to another:

Boom. The footage fumes. Once
upon a time there was a suicide. Once upon a time

there was an affair & a missile, a mis-
understanding, an intervention, a   *B-*

Bomb, bomb, bomb, bomb, bomb, bomb, bomb—
Keep mouthing after the newscaster moves on.

                        Ka-
Boom: a fourteen year old girl married a bomb.

REPORT FROM THE DAUGHTER OF A BLUE PLANET

Night after night the land
delivers its verdict. Blades
of grass struggle through earth,
hearts & lungs develop in their sacs.
Beetles mingle with dust & buds
of flowers unfasten for the last time.
The man convicted as a child

will perish. The future
accumulates its matter beneath
the surface of life going
about its business. The mind
dissembles & covers itself with sleep.
from a distance we measure
the moon, but might not
recognize our own children.
A woman calls across a continent
& no one answers.

GINGIVITIS, NOTES ON FEAR

I hesitate invoking that
my daughter's mouth
not her first vanity
she tastes & smoothes
her chin this way & that,
bones replacing the fallen.
it repairs itself: two
  forming new words:
    brushing past

doubled emptiness: open—
in the bathroom mirror—
but first blood inkling
with her tongue. She turns
anticipating her future: new
If the body survives,
pillars—wider, stronger
  adolescent declarations
    seasoned gums

What is the tongue-
between trauma &
Incident &

span
terror?
accident?

Think

on these things.

There is so much to *fear*.

How will we *fear* it all?

& now my second-born,

my son: If I don't

brush, he says,

a disease will attack my gums.

The Riot Inside Me

King's body swallowed   then released   a black
boy's spirit
      a bullet   a son
grazes the earth
every black hand   reached   someone said   an
incurable urge to fly
      in the neighborhood   a weapon
maybe
clutched something
sacred
       blades of grass
     some of us took   our future
sparks
the streets   live again   even in
flame

Communion with Mary Lou Williams

Tender-headed, cold-blooded, uncorrupt—
                    I rush
& gather   & stitch   them   up
your   flats &   bents

&   low   dwelling notes
onto   my sleeves   & onto   my   skirts

your music has tailored a lovely coat

&

*

I've learned to pray
                    through my fingertips—

*

Dear Composer, Dear Mother, Dear Daughter of the Elusive, Dear
Black Coffee, Dear Ambition, Dear Confidence, Dear Zoning, Dear
Doubt, Dear Absence, Dear Comeback, Dear Plays Like a Man, Dear
Chez Mary Lou, Dear Daring, Dear Rosary in the Palm, Dear Twelve
Bars over Dishes Clanking, Dear Muse, Dear Majesty, Dear Live at

the Cookery, Dear Sinner in Search of a Saint, Dear Suckled Breast,
Dear Ornery, Dear Ornate, Dear Obstacle, Dear Orchid, Dear Ostrich
Feather in a Cap, Dear Thrift Store Owner, Dear Shoes from Lucille
Armstrong, Dear Mink Bowtie from Ellington, Dear Matron of
Music, Dear Soup for Musicians, Dear Holy Spirit, Dear Glory, Dear
Daughter of the Imperfect Mother,

*

Give me one good reason
        to fool with you, to roll em & roll em—
these down-home notes, these
parts of me, you
        hip cats, you wannabes, you running men
& wandering women, you Jesus children.
Imagine strolling New York streets
        with the stretch-marked sounds
of bass & trill, the labor
of music in a childless body
        sacrificed to the service of
America's Holy Music & all
the ancestors with their rattling
        of bones in the traffic & cursing,
their voices nudging callused feet
forward two blocks, two blocks more
        past all the people trying

to get right. To get right
is to get with Memphis & Mississippi.
            If you wanna boogie
                  with me, you gotta get right
with the Giver of Blues.

*

Reverend Williams—
what Miles Davis called you
behind your back.

What you wanted was
a low-down connection.
Boogie-woogie promise
of call & response. Music
joined with spirit like the ball
& socket of a swinging hip.

You listened to the music slip
further from muddy water like
a country man suffering
in a new bright suit.

*

44

Wooden crosses & rosary beads
Jazz created through suffering . . . .

*

A lover nudges the ghost
from my right breast, nipple
plucked in quiet light.
I can't escape what lurks
beneath skin, further back
than blood & bone, this sex
this music & another
I don't remember. Tonight
is the Gatekeeper of Memory.

I struggle to be let in.
Who protects me? I
dare the ghost forward. Or is it
the God of Hard-Crossed Hands
always watching? No. Someone else
has been here, my flinched face
confesses. Who? You?

*

You did or you didn't or would not do.
Call it grace or luck, a devil's deal,
a girl defying her mother.

Little Dove Child? Niña Naive?
To: You-Know-Who?
From: You-Know-Who?

*

Is to love
to be born in the name of to die in the name of to be blessed in the name
of to question love in the name of to question the name in the name of
to name names in the name of the name of naming love

The Shape the Water Takes

Sound—Part 3 (Ostinato): All the World's Wars Commence in the Head

Hunched in a thimble, I wept. *Mercy.*
Once blotted out trees. *Well.*
Made some second-guess me. *Speak.*
Ought not act so ugly.
Said—
Ought not act so ugly.
Hunched in a thimble, I wept. *Yes, yes.*
Won't make no apologies. *Naw, Sir.*
Who will take on this burden?
Ought not walk alone.
Said—
Ought not walk alone.
In my sleep, I wandered.
Sssssssssssssss stitch, sssssssssssssss stitch,
Sssssssssssssss stitch, sssssssssssssss stitch,
Sssssssssssssss stitch.
That's the way they do you.
Said—
That's the way they do you.
Words can make a mountain.
Said—
Words can make a mountain.
No pulpits in the thimble.
Said—
No pulpits in the thimble.
Head—hah—
Head—hah—
Said—

Head, shoulders, knees & legwork.
Ought not act so ugly.
Ought not act so ugly.
Head, shoulders, knees & legwork.
No room for one more.
No room for one more.
Don't go pray for me.
Don't go pray for me.
No acres for want in a thimble.
Said—
No acres for want in a thimble.
All I could do was roll.
Said—
All I could do was roll. *Mm-hmm.*
Sssssssssssssss stitch, sssssssssssssss stitch,
Sssssssssssssss stitch, sssssssssssssss stitch,
Sssssssssssssss stitch?
I know not what, I know not what.

MARY J. (UPSWING)

The booth had a door & the table had a door & the cup
had a door & the darkness had a door you fell right through,
you song in the head of a heathen. Someone had
penciled your skirt, someone had lengthened your legs,
someone had softened your bangs. & someone had drawn
a mic & a door with a stage light peering through. & someone flipped
the pages so your legs moved & your knees knocked &
though your stiletto heels bent, they didn't break or get dirty.
You were all motion & muscle moving with the logic of women
who float in teacups. Closed door, open door, cracked door, hidden
door, crate door, the door to heaven? You Yonkers lament, you
unlatched the little leaves fastened around your ankles
& swished your way to the surface, a song in your mouth,
a pattern in your hair. You breath in the break when we swim.

NERUDA

Memory—
      What we accept without wanting to   *A certain weariness*

The birth   *How much happens in a day*
                The first journey   *We are too many*
The first sea
           Dazzle of day   *Too many names*
Sex
               Shyness   *Forgotten in autumn*
Superstitions

There is no clear light   *Strangers on the shore*
               Look to the market   *The friend returns*

To those at odds   *Not quite so tall*
                The abandoned   *And how long?*

The lost child   *A dream of trains*
          The long day called
    Thursday   *A letter ordering lumber*
                     Poor boys
Oh, my lost city   *Galloping in the South*
                   Keeping quiet
               My people

My crazy friends
                    Maybe we have
        time   Through a closed mouth the flies enter
                                        And the city has gone
I remember the East
            The night train
October fullness   The old woman of the shore
        Soliloquy in the waves   Memories and weeks
That night   Furious struggle between seamen and
                        an octopus
                    Insomnia   of colossal size
The fisherman
                The wicked king
Perhaps I've changed since then   Oh, such bottomless Saturdays!
                    First travelings
Loves
        Lost letters
Books   This is where we live

        Those lives   Emerging
The forest
            The hunter in the forest

Goodbye to the snow
             The school of winter   *Here, there, everywhere*

At last there is no one
                          The future is space   *Consequences*
Solitude
                 Cruel fire   *At last they have gone*

It is not necessary   *I ask for silence*
           Spring in the city   *Daylight with night key*
                                                  It happened in winter

One Impression

The American flag doesn't really wave
or say goodbye or goodnight but reminds
my neighbor her husband was once
here raising the colors she raises now.
He's gone like Nabokov's blues lifted
as if they'd never known chrysalis struggle,
entering the world of air & atrocities
tucked in pockets or in the folds of scarves
at the backs of drawers where the forgotten
never soundly rest, but awaken when brushed.
Of course, they're here in the steel, in the threads
of white folded gloves, in the ground, in the y

& y & y & y his widow's broom makes sweeping
the handicapped space where his car used to wait.

Devil Music

When I was waiting for my son to be born, I dreamt he would
turn to stone & I would drop him. He'd come out gray &
chiseled with angst, or whatever fear the Devil likes to watch
a woman wrestle while the Devil sits back, humpbacked,
crooked-letter backed, stirring his morning coffee.

Not that I believe in the Devil.

Though he did get hold of me one night, planting that stone
baby in my crib & filling the cracks of its cheeks with blood.
What did it mean? What did it mean? I worried until my real boy arrive
fleshy & intact. I draped the child in spikes & armor. & sealed
his room with a hundred questions. To be let in, one had to
ask the right questions.

Then, as was customary, the old Devil found a new head to haunt,
    probably
another woman's, this time, expecting a girl.
O, the Devil is nothing if not judicious in his industry.
Or so it seemed.

Until. Until. Until. Until. Until. Until.

O, you know, the Devil comes a calling. Though
I do not believe in him.

O, you know, the Devil comes a calling. Though
I do not believe in him.

His flicking fallen stars from his teeth, his suitcase
dented with gravel, his boots on the table, his pound
of sugar, his pint of cream, his leaning back, humpbacked,
crooked-letter backed, stirring his noontime tea.

You always tune me out, he says.
Like when I play Dylan for you.
You never listen when I play Dylan for you.

& that's his trick, his truth & lie. His accusation & his whine.
His decent taste in music. It's true sometimes, a sound
won't fit, the voice, the pitch, too scratchy, too low.
With a boy who'd been nursed & kept intact,
time was not easily given. Then, in walked my boy

with the Devil's coat, a long, black coat
I'd never noticed, signaling time for the Devil to go.
& after the Devil had gone, my boy said:
I dreamt of my aunt, your sister, last night.

She fell & cracked & turned to birds,
a thousand birds like covered songs.

She fell & cracked & turned to birds,
a thousand birds like covered songs.

My sister who'd been up three nights straight.
O, you know, a suitor came a calling. He kept asking her
out & out & out, though she didn't dance much anymore.
Let's cut a few rugs, he said.
We'll listen to music & lift ourselves up.
Though she did not believe him.

Until. Until. Until. Until. Until. Until.

She was tired. She was so so tired.
She wondered how he was able to reach her.
Her voicemail was full, her phone was unplugged,
& she couldn't hear the doorbell when washing
the laundry. She was always washing the laundry.

O, you know, the Devil comes a calling.
Though I do not believe in him.

His boat with one oar, his music that floats,
his quilts for the weary, how he whispers,
Lie back, with his humpbacked back, his
crooked-letter back, stirring his sundown tonic.

O, you know, the Devil comes a calling.
But I do not believe in him.

THEORY OF THE UNHELD

"The old brain cannot solve the enormous problem of living."
    —J. Krishnamurti

you   break
  can   yourself

before   break
    they   you

broken   dusk
    against

without   or   change
  glances regret

what couldn't
    you

dust nickels minted
  beneath   newly

        all

you do
  must is

      swipe hands
        your

or so

acknowledged at the podium of certain beliefs

some fists
    pound

some shatter
  palms

why is face the face
  your

that makes
  the others

falter?

they were expecting

someone else

someone ^{more}

talkative ^{more} serious ^{more}

serene perhaps
someone

more someone
needy not
broken

before ^{they} break
you

Brilliance

Sometimes you find yourself
facing it, after
early July approximations
have fizzled on
an urban patch
of green or sidewalk or down
at the Riverfront you
wisely avoided.

"Our Radiant Light,"
said The Stone.

(True that, true that).
But who on Earth can stand it?
To be brilliant, but always
questioning the gift,
its smart, black packaging:

(What grace is
wrapped this way?)

Before you
know it, it's in
your skin, your kin, your bone:

I don't know, you
keep saying. But
you do—no—
Dammit, you don't.

Black Winged Stilt

When God says, "Meet me tomorrow
at the corner of Seventh Day & Salvation
just as the sun before nightfall strikes
the fender of a red hatchback parked
outside Worldwide Washateria," you

wait there
fitted in a dress the color of cloud-cover
& hold a feathered hat
to your delicate hair, newly picked &
haloed with a small brim. &

like a fleck of Antique Black in a gallon
of European White, you make everything

around you
more
like itself, which means you
appear

more
eloquently than the lampposts
boasting their specters of light,

or the woman
clutching her daughter's shirt
above a basket, the sedative twilight
of the gods trapped momentarily

in the pane, which separate
the woman
& you

steadfast against the wind picking up,
the men desiring your attention,
the traffic held
in the ceaseless straight ahead.

Concrete barriers, a few
lopsided cones, abiding
highway hieroglyphs
are all that separate
onward & stalled, here & gone.

Not even this poem
can move you, or change

the motion of your scarf—
that furious red flag—
or the stilts—your legs.
Your lips

don't move—you
do not mutter or
complain or ask directions.

Why don't you?
Your autograph haunts
the covers of books
across town:

I know who I am I know who I am I know who I am
You,

Black-winged bird,
you've become
lyrics layering air:

1—
Describe the sound of His voice.

2—
To walk the black, wired bars

3—
is to follow a sound

1—
so peculiar you

2—
hardly notice

3—
the ink gone out.

1—
2- 3- 1- 2- 3- 1- 2- 3- 1-

Your stilts on the ground.

MEDITATION ON YOUR ESCAPE

Little portal to the Underworld.
Or the World Overhead, depending.
Your disappearance overwhelms me.
What were you saying with one small plea
in an otherwise empty letter?
If only I'd replied: *You are not broken.*
Whatever feels broken, we can repair.

*

Who to keep out, who to let in?
This is the dilemma.
Disasters aside,
let us consider air & light.
How much, how much, how much?

*

We viewed you through so many
primary colors. You were
so still you shook us
with the secret of your teeth & eyes.

Open-Toed Shoes

FIGURE 1.

Shoes worn once [with collapse intuited]. (A) Heel [2.5 inches, wooden, faux]. I'd never fallen—on a stage, on a sidewalk, in a bad relationship—never. Not a single heartbreak. Sneakers & sandals, tomboy wanderer. Method: stay low to the ground. [The break would wait] plus: (B) Toes [absent]. Bent from too small shoes, from too small budgets, from a too long childhood. (C) & here one must step outside the figure. & here one must leap [dream signs, dream visions, & so forth]. Full grown, I landed in Houston & shopped with a man [not shown]. *You look so different,* I said to him. There was blue between us. *Those shoes?* he asked when I lifted them. *Yes,* I said & slipped them on [yes to their blue dusk straps, yes to the box, to the bag, & yes to figuring where to wear them].

FIGURE 2.

April. The space where one —. [& is led]. Intuit, intuit, intuit. *She fell,* they answered when I asked what happened. & one week later into the grove she went while I stood in these shoes [these shoes].

THE SHAPE COMPASSION TAKES

Until a moment ago Möbius bands were great fish
        chanting in water, the sound of Möbius
more hypnotic than paper striving to be infinite & classic
like famous whales or wannabe singers. & then I turned
        my head to a page in a book. I was 11 or 12.
It was a lesson on the verb "to be" or it was a lesson
about creation. I was 16 or 17. What did I know
        about DNA or the birthplaces of King, Gandhi, or Sappho?
How quickly can you locate Atlanta, Porbandar, or Lesbos on a map?
I tried to resist puritanical answers. I tried to trust
what my head could accomplish. I was 19 or 21.
        I wasn't ignoring the elephant in the room, but gazing upon
its magnificent toenails, the fossilized history between them.
I was 27 or 28. I spoke often to myself:
In an emergent process, two is more
than twice as many as one.
        Do not fear this idea: there was you
born to a certain family of a certain city.
And then there was you
        becoming another woman entirely,
speaking in the antelope's voice.
 Or was it the jackal's?
        When a herd mourns a fallen calf in the plain,
the youngest survivor circles back to bless her sister.
She suspects the body will take the form of a dragonfly
        or maybe the shape compassion takes.
You can speak of this if you want.
Give yourself permission.

It's hard to know, it's hard not to
loop back toward those daydream-inspired turns at the front
of a storm-colored school room, where no one,
            not even the teacher, was listening.
I was 33 or 34. I wanted God, I wanted science,
to predict, explain, intervene,
but she couldn't or he wouldn't or it wouldn't, and so
            I sat, not paralyzed, but something like it, lukewarm
on gospel, a loose shell in a tambourine, waiting for rapture.

In Toni Morrison's Head

White girls die first.
Which means I'm still
alive, but breathless &
on the run in the brain's
maze of scrutiny. How
I stumble in the memory
of Ohio, old names & faces
given me: Pecola, Dorcas,
Violet, Nel, First Corinthians.
Reinvention is my birthright.
With each step I am altered:
mother, daughter, river, sun. A tree
swells on my dark back
& no one waits in the future to
kiss me, only the towns-
women hissing at my
inappropriate dress, but not
at the sweet-talking rogue
who travels with me.
Inside the mire my heart
still pulses at first, fatigued
& deathbound, then quick.
There's not enough milk
for all these babies or
the blue-eyed dolls yanking
their mouths open & shut.
Give a little clap, clap, clap,
chant the children & there's some-

thing ancient about the music's call
to order. *(Put them in your lap.)*
Who wouldn't stop to trace
the scars on the walls, their
embroidery of skin, stitches
that stretch for miles? *Not I,*
says the Jolly Old Woman
disappearing in a warm tunnel,
asking, *Toni, won't you tell me
a funny story?* I cut my losses
& sprint. I'm smoke, I'm ash,
Holy Ghost & Crucifix,
the preacher reborn to a body
in the grass, chirping, *Death
is so much different than I imagined.*

Sound—Part 4: Notes on Polyphony

At first I felt my head was too much with me. *Take it off*, I heard a voice say. *Your head, you got to take it off.* So I closed my eyes & took my head by the ears & turned. It came off easy. My head. Like all my life it was waiting for me to unscrew it. So I sat it down quietly beside me. & this allowed my mouth—which all before had been sewed shut—to open & sing. *What have I to dread? What have I to fear?* & my hips, torso, & upright arms trembled at that sudden a cappella. I want to thank you for hearing this small trickle in a sea. I am trying to steady myself as I wait. There's a bored shark coloring the water. There's a girl cradling her head somewhere. She is lost & someone has left her at the shore without a song, without a whistle. There is only her blood & the blood of her siblings. There is only the sun like the glimmer of the State's buttons erasing the girl. You have placed her in my throat. & now I can reattach my head. & the girl is inside me; she can move now as my body moves, my neck, my head nodding.

NOTES

The Ruth Stone epigraph comes from Yvonne Daley's article "These Enormous Simplicities: A Profile of Ruth Stone" in *Poets & Writers* (Sept./Oct. 2004).

The Mary Lou Williams epigraph comes from the biography, *Morning Glory*, by Linda Dahl (Pantheon Books, 1999). Tammy L. Kernoodle also wrote a significant biography, *Soul on Soul*, about Williams.

"Report from the Daughter of a Blue Planet" is for Napoleon Beazley.

The Krishnamurti quotation is taken from *Freedom from the Known*.

"[Zodiac Suite]" takes it title from Mary Lou Williams's piano composition of the same name. Williams's project with the Zodiac Suite was to compose songs that corresponded with the astrological signs of some of her fellow musician friends. The poems in this series mimic Williams's ambitious and loving process. The poems are both public and private centos, elegies, and odes.

Epigraphs in "Sound—Part 2: Hearing My Daughter's Heartbeat the First Time" are taken from *The Essential Etheridge Knight* ("Ilu, The Talking Drum") *Thieves of Paradise* ("Ode to the Drum"), and from *Jonah's Gourde Vine*.

"The Antelope as Document" takes its name from Michael Buckland's essay "What is a 'Document,'" in which Buckland discusses French librarian Suzanne Briet who wrote, "[a] document is evidence in support of a fact." The italicized words are Briet's writings.

"Neruda" is a cento composed of poem titles from Pablo Neruda's *La Extravagaria* and *Isla Negra*, Alastair Reid, translator.

Acknowledgments

Many thanks to the editors who first published some of these poems (some in different versions):

5 AM, Bat City Review, Callaloo, Crab Orchard Review, Gulf Coast, The Journal, jubilat, No Tell Motel, The Owl Project, Ploughshares, Poem Memoir Story, Rattle, and *West Branch.*

"In Toni Morrison's Head" and "Blessing Blue Crabs" were archived at *The Fishouse Online Audio Archive.* "In Toni Morrison's Head" was anthologized in *Gathering Ground: A Reader Celebrating Cave Canem's First Decade.* "Mother, Love" also appeared in *The Autumn House Anthology of Contemporary American Poetry,* 2nd ed. "Sound—Part 2: Hearing My Daughter's Heartbeat the First Time" also appeared in *A Poet's Craft: A Comprehensive Guide to Making and Sharing Your Poetry.*

Deepest gratitude to my husband and children for their love, support, and care over the many years this book was written, set aside, and rewritten.

Thank you, Carol Muske-Dukes, for championing this book in its earliest, quietest stages. Thanks to Sally Ball, Martha Rhodes, and Ryan Murphy for your guidance during the production of this book. Thank you, Maya Freelon Asante.

For their careful readings of these poems at various times, I thank Douglas Kearney, Shara McCallum, and Terrance Hayes.

Many thanks to Toi Derricotte, Cornelius Eady, and the people of Cave Canem.

Thank you, Crystal Williams, for everything.

Born in southern Ohio, Yona Harvey is a literary artist residing in Pittsburgh, Pennsylvania. She has received a Barbara Deming Award, an Individual Artist Grant from The Pittsburgh Foundation, a Pittsburgh Flight School Fellowship, and a Virginia Center for the Creative Arts Fellowship. *Hemming the Water* is her first book. More information can be found at www.yonaharvey.com.